MW00815150

Bible Lessons to Grow By

Christian Virtues
Made Fun and Easy!

PreK–K

By
Jeanette Dall

Cover art by
Laura Merer

Inside illustrations by
Chris Wold Dyrud

Publisher
In Celebration™
a division of Ideal • Instructional Fair Publishing Group
Grand Rapids, Michigan 49544

Dear Parents, Teachers, and Children,

This book is designed for parents and children to do together. The Bible stories are written in the vocabulary and to the interest of 3–5 year olds. The activities are varied and include fingerplays, songs, crafts, and simple pencil games. All the activities can be completed by the children with a minimum of adult help.

Each lesson emphasizes a character-building value. These values are shown in the life and actions of the Bible-time person portrayed. An application of that value to the child's life is also introduced. The lessons are arranged chronologically but may be used in any order.

"From infancy, you have known the holy Scriptures,
which are able to make you wise for salvation
through faith in Christ Jesus"
(2 Timothy 3:15).

Copyright Notice

In Celebration™ grants the right to the individual purchaser to reproduce patterns and student activity materials in this book for noncommercial individual or classroom use only. Reproduction for an entire school or school system is strictly prohibited. No other part of this publication may be reproduced in whole or in part. No part of this publication may be reproduced for storage in a retrieval system or transmitted in any form or by any means, electronic, mechanical, recording, or otherwise, without the prior written permission of the publisher. For information regarding permission write to: In Celebration, P.O. Box 1650, Grand Rapids, MI 49501.

Scripture taken from the HOLY BIBLE: NEW INTERNATIONAL VERSION®. NIV®. Copyright © 1973, 1978, 1984 by International Bible Society. Used by permission of Zondervan Publishing House.

The "NIV" and "New International Version" trademarks are registered in the United States Patent and Trademark Office by International Bible Society.

Credits:
Author: Jeanette Dall
Cover Illustrator: Laura Merer
Inside Illustrations: Chris Wold Dyrud
Project Director: Alyson Kieda
Editors: Linda Triemstra, Sara Dillbeck
Text Design: Deborah Hanson McNiff

About the Author:
Jeanette Dall received a Bachelor of Arts in Education from Concordia University. Jeanette has 23 years experience teaching preschool through grade 4. She has been active in her church as a Sunday school, VBS, and adult class teacher. Jeanette also has extensive editing and writing experience.

Standard Book Number: 1-56822-814-7
Bible Lessons to Grow By: Christian Virtues Made Fun and Easy (PreK–K)
Copyright © 1999 by In Celebration™
Ideal • Instructional Fair Publishing Group
a division of Tribune Education
2400 Turner Avenue NW
Grand Rapids, Michigan 49544

All Rights Reserved • Printed in the USA

Table of Contents

1.
God Made People
Genesis 1:26–2:25

God made the whole world and everything in it. God made the sky and the land. He made lakes, oceans, and rivers. God put the sun, the moon, and all the stars in the sky.

God made every kind of plant. God made all the fish that swim in the ocean and the animals that walk on the land. God made the birds that fly in the sky. The world God made was very good.

Then God was ready to make someone very special. God wanted to make someone to take care of the world. So God made people.

First God made a man. God called the man Adam. God put Adam in a beautiful garden. Many trees and plants grew there. Many animals lived there too. God wanted Adam to take care of all the plants and animals.

God did not want Adam to live alone. So God made a woman. Adam named the woman Eve. God was very pleased with Adam and Eve. They could talk with God and be friends with him. Adam and Eve were happy in the world God made.

Memory Verse
"I praise you because I am . . . wonderfully made" (Psalm 139:14).

To Talk About
God makes boys and girls special too. What are some special things about you?

Prayer
Dear God, thank you for making the world. Thank you for making me special. Help me to love you and to take care of the world. Amen.

Special Me!

What you need:
small paper plate
colored markers
pencil
hair-colored yarn
scissors
glue
large craft stick

What you do:
1. Use a pencil to draw a mouth, nose, and eyes on the paper plate.
2. Color the eyes on the plate to match your eye color.
3. Choose yarn to match your hair color. Cut the yarn in pieces and glue to the paper plate to look like hair.
4. Glue a craft stick to the back of the plate. Use the stick for a handle.
5. Write "God made (your name)" on the handle.

How you can use it:
1. Use the puppet to tell how God made the world and people.
2. Use the puppet to tell someone how God made you special.

© In Celebration™

IF9560 *Christian Virtues (PreK-K)*

Noah Obeys God

Genesis 6:9–9:17

A long time ago, the people of the world did not love or obey God. Only Noah and his family still loved God. One day, God told Noah to build a very big boat. The boat was called an ark. God would send lots and lots of rain. It would cover the whole world. But God would keep Noah and his family and two of every kind of animal safe in the ark.

Noah obeyed God. He and his sons built the ark. It took a long, long time. When the ark was done, they filled it with food.

God called the animals to the ark and Noah helped them on. Then Noah and his family went into the ark too. God shut the big, big doors. God said, "Don't be afraid. I will protect you."

Down came the rain for 40 days and 40 nights. Water covered everything. Noah had to wait a very long time before he could see dry land. Then Noah opened the doors and went out.

Noah and his family thanked God for keeping all of them safe. Then God put a big, beautiful rainbow in the sky. God said, "I promise never to send a flood to cover the whole earth again."

Memory Verse
"Noah did everything just as God commanded him" (Genesis 6:22).

To Talk About
How did Noah obey God? How can you obey God?

Prayer
Almighty God, I'm glad you saved Noah and his family. I like seeing beautiful rainbows. Help me obey you, just as Noah did. Amen.

Noah and the Flood

Sing this song to the tune of "Are You Sleeping?" Make up actions to go with the words.

1. Noah obeyed
    Noah obeyed
    Built an ark
    Built an ark
    Just as God had told him
    Just as God had told him
    It was big!
    It was big!

2. The animals came
    The animals came
    Two by two
    Two by two
    Everyone was safe now
    Everyone was safe now
    In the ark
    In the ark.

3. Then it rained
    Then it rained
    Forty days
    Forty nights
    Everything was covered
    Everything was covered
    By the flood
    By the flood.

4. The flood dried up
    The flood dried up
    Thank you, God
    Thank you, God
    God made a bright rainbow
    God made a bright rainbow
    In the sky
    In the sky.

3.
Abram Has Faith

Genesis 12:1-9; 15:1-6

Abram loved God very much. God loved Abram too. One day, God told Abram about a special plan. God said, "Go to a faraway land to live." He didn't even tell Abram the name of the land. God said he would show Abram the way. Abram had faith and believed what God said.

Abram took his family and everything they had and started out on a long trip. The loads on the camels' backs swayed with each step. Clunk-clunkity-clunk went the cooking pots. Sheep ran here and there.

Clunk-clunkity-clunk. Day after day they kept going until finally they arrived! The land where God led them was called Canaan. The people in Canaan didn't believe in God. And the people had powerful armies. But Abram had faith and trusted God to take care of him.

God made Abram a promise. He said that someday Abram's great-grandchildren would own this beautiful land. God also promised Abram many other blessings. Before the camels were unloaded and tents set up, Abram was busy building an altar to God. It was only a few rocks piled on top of each other, but it reminded Abram of God's promises. Then Abram thanked and worshiped God.

Memory Verse
"Abram believed the LORD"
(Genesis 15:6).

To Talk About
How did Abram show he had faith in God? How does God care for you?

Prayer
Dear God, thank you for taking care of me just as you took care of Abram. Help me to have faith in you and to trust you, as Abram did. Amen.

A Long Trip

Abram and all the people with him had to take a long trip. God took care of them and told them where to go. Help Abram find the land of Canaan.

4.
Jacob's Dream
Genesis 28:10–22

Jacob tricked his father into giving him the family blessing. That blessing belonged to Jacob's brother, Esau. Esau became very angry and wanted to hurt Jacob. So Jacob ran away.

At night, Jacob was tired and wanted to sleep, so he lay down on the ground and used a big stone for a pillow. While he slept, Jacob had a dream. In his dream, he saw a long stairway. The stairway reached from the ground all the way up to heaven. Angels went up and down the stairway.

At the top of the stairway was God. Jacob heard God say, "I am the Lord, God of your grandfather and your father. One day I will give the land you are lying on to the people in your family."

God made Jacob another promise. He said, "I will be with you, wherever you go. I will not leave you. I will keep my promises to you."

Then Jacob woke up and he felt afraid. He knew that this place was special. Jacob said, "God is here! This is God's house."

The next morning, Jacob got up early. He poured oil on the stone that he had used for a pillow. He named the place Bethel. Bethel means "house of God."

Memory Verse
"[Jacob] thought, 'Surely the LORD is in this place'" (Genesis 28:16).

To Talk About
What did Jacob see and hear in his dream? How did Jacob show he loved God? How can you show you love God?

Prayer
Heavenly Father, you promised to take care of Jacob. Thank you for taking care of me too. Help me to show love to you just as Jacob did. Amen.

Angels Watching Over Me

God promised to take care of Jacob. Angels watched over him. Angels watch over you too. Color this angel. You can add glitter or stickers to make it look extra special.

5.

Joseph Forgives

Genesis 37; 41:41–47:12

Jacob had twelve sons. But Jacob loved his son Joseph more than his other sons. Jacob made a special, fancy coat for Joseph. When Joseph's brothers saw it, they were jealous and angry. They sold Joseph to some men who took him far away to Egypt.

God was with Joseph in Egypt. After many years, the king put Joseph in charge of Egypt. Joseph told the people to save food when the crops were good. The food was stored in big barns. When food stopped growing because no rain fell, Joseph sold the food stored in the barns.

One day, ten of Joseph's brothers came to buy food. Joseph knew who they were, but they didn't know Joseph. Joseph sold them food, and they went home. When they had eaten all the food, Joseph's brothers came back.

Joseph welcomed his brothers and had a special dinner for them. Later Joseph said, "I am your brother, Joseph." The brothers were very afraid that Joseph would be angry with them.

But Joseph could tell his brothers were sorry for what they had done to him. Joseph put his arms around them. He said, "I forgive you. God wanted me here to keep our family alive."

Memory Verse
"Forgive as the Lord forgave you" (Colossians 3:13).

To Talk About

Why did the brothers go to Egypt? How did the brothers feel when Joseph told them who he was? What did Joseph say to his brothers? What can you do when someone is mean to you?

Prayer

Dear God, thank you for forgiving me. Help me to forgive others, just as Joseph forgave his brothers. Amen.

Joseph and His Brothers

What you need:
2 or more toilet paper tubes
fabric scraps
scissors
glue
markers
white construction paper

What you do:
1. Use the end of the tube to trace circles (one per tube) onto the white paper. Cut out the circles. Make happy faces and hair on the circles.

2. Put glue all over the outside of the tubes. Cut the fabric into strips and glue it onto the tubes.

3. Glue a face at the top of each tube. Put a crown on one head. Set the puppets aside to dry.

How you can use it:
1. Hold the puppet by putting one or two fingers inside the tube. You can hold more than one puppet by putting one on each hand.

2. Pretend the puppet with the crown is Joseph. The other puppet is one of his brothers.

3. Use the puppets to tell the story of Joseph forgiving his brothers.

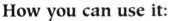

6.

Miriam Helps Her Baby Brother

Exodus 2:1-10

Miriam and her family were Hebrew slaves. Miriam had a baby brother. She wanted to help her mother hide the baby from the bad king. The king had ordered all Hebrew baby boys to be killed.

Mother made a basket bed for the baby. It was like a little boat. Mother put the baby in the basket. Then she and Miriam took the basket bed to the river and put it in the water. "We will hide the baby here," Mother said. "Maybe someone will find him."

Miriam stayed nearby and watched to make sure the baby was safe. Soon Miriam saw some women. It was the princess and her helpers. "What's in that basket?" the princess asked her helpers. One of them went to get the basket. When the princess looked inside, the baby began to cry.

Then Miriam ran to the princess. "Shall I get someone to help take care of the baby?" Miriam asked.

The princess said, "Yes."

Then Miriam ran to get her mother. The princess told Mother to take care of the baby. "I will call the baby Moses," said the princess.

Memory Verse
"His sister stood at a distance to see what would happen to him" (Exodus 2:4).

To Talk About
Why did the baby have to be hidden? How did Miriam help her brother? How can you help someone?

Prayer
Thank you for taking care of me, God. Let me think of ways that I can help other people. Amen.

The Basket Bed

Connect the dots to make a basket bed for Miriam's baby brother. Then you can color the picture.

7.

Gideon Knows God Will Help

Judges 6:7–7:21

Gideon was a farmer. He had picked his wheat and was hiding it from his enemies. Enemies had taken his grain and the grain of many other farmers before. So Gideon and the other people prayed. They asked God for help.

An angel came to Gideon and said, "God will show you what to do. He will help you fight your enemies."

Gideon called the men in his land. He told them what the angel said. Many men came to fight. But God told Gideon, "There are too many men. Send home the ones that are scared." Then God said, "You still have too many men."

More men went home. Finally there were only 300 men left. Then God told Gideon to fight the enemies at night. Gideon knew God would help them defeat their enemies.

Each man had a trumpet and a torch hidden inside a jar. While the enemies were sleeping, Gideon and the men stood all around their camp. Then they blew the trumpets and broke the jars. What a noise! And so many fires! The enemies were terrified. They ran away.

Gideon and his people were safe again.

Memory Verse
"If God is for us, who can be against us?" (Romans 8:31).

To Talk About
How many men were left to fight the enemies? Why was Gideon not afraid? What are some things God does for you?

Prayer
Almighty God, you can do anything. Help me to know you can always help me, no matter what happens. Amen.

Gideon's Soldiers

Six of Gideon's soldiers are hiding in this picture. Draw a circle around each one.

8.
Ruth and Naomi
Ruth 1–4

Naomi had left her home many years ago with her husband and sons. Then Naomi's husband and her sons died. Naomi had only her daughter-in-law Ruth to help her.

Naomi was going back to her old home. Ruth wanted to go with her. Naomi said, "You don't need to leave your home and go with me."

Ruth loved Naomi and respected her. She said, "I want to help you. Your family will be my family. And your God will be my God."

After many days, Ruth and Naomi arrived at Naomi's old home. Naomi's friends were happy to see her. They were glad Ruth would take care of her.

Naomi and Ruth were very poor. They didn't have enough money to buy food. So Ruth went to a field where the harvesters were cutting the grain. Ruth walked behind them and picked up the grain that dropped or was left over. Naomi used the grain to make food.

Boaz owned the field of grain. He told Ruth, "You may take all the leftover grain you need because you are so kind to Naomi."

Later Ruth and Boaz got married. They asked Naomi to live with them.

Memory Verse
"Where you go I will go, and where you stay I will stay" (Ruth 1:16).

To Talk About
Why did Ruth want to leave her home to go with Naomi? How did Ruth show love for Naomi? How do you show love for someone?

Prayer
Loving God, I'm glad you love me. I love you too. Help me to be loving and respectful to others, just as Ruth was to Naomi. Amen.

Gathering Grain

Ruth is picking up leftover grain in Boaz's field. Help Ruth fill her basket. Draw a line from the leftover grain to Ruth's basket.

9.
Samuel Listens
I Samuel 3:1-19

When Samuel was a little boy, he went to live in the temple. Samuel served God by helping the priest, Eli. Eli taught Samuel about working in the temple. He explained God's Word to Samuel. Samuel learned many things about God.

One night when Samuel was in his bed, he heard someone call him. Samuel thought it was Eli. So Samuel went to Eli's room. But Eli said, "I didn't call you. Go back to bed."

Samuel went back to bed. Once again he heard a voice call, "Samuel!"

Samuel thought, "It must be Eli." But no, Eli had not called him. So Samuel went back to bed.

Samuel heard the voice a third time. He went to Eli again. Now Eli knew God was calling Samuel. Eli told Samuel, "Go back to bed. The next time, tell God you are listening."

Samuel went back to bed. God called, "Samuel! Samuel!"

Samuel said, "I'm listening, Lord." Samuel listened to all that God said. The next morning Samuel told Eli everything. Samuel kept on listening to God and obeying him as he grew up.

Memory Verse
"Then Samuel said, 'Speak, for your servant is listening'" (1 Samuel 3:10).

To Talk About
Who called Samuel? How did Samuel answer? How do you know what God wants you to do?

Prayer
Dear God, thank you for giving me family and other grown-ups who can teach me about you. Help me to listen carefully, just as Samuel did. Amen.

Listening Game

Listen carefully to the sounds on the audio cassette. Can you tell what they are?

What you need:
blank audio cassette
cassette player
familiar sounds—fire engine shrieking, teakettle whistling, dog barking, doorbell buzzing, baby crying, telephone ringing, door slamming, car engine starting, vacuum cleaner, water running or dripping, ball bouncing

What you do:
1. Have an adult record 8 to 10 sounds, leaving a 10–15 second pause between sounds. Use the sounds suggested above or others of your choice.
2. Listen carefully as the audio cassette is played.
3. Play the sounds one at a time. See how many you can identify.

10.

David Is Chosen

1 Samuel 16:1-13

David was a shepherd boy. He took very good care of his father's sheep. David always watched over the sheep and knew where they were. He found good grass and water for the sheep and kept them from getting lost. David also protected the sheep from wild animals. He helped them when they were hurt. Many times while David watched the sheep, he sang songs of praise to God.

One day, Samuel came to see David's father, Jesse. God had told Samuel that one of Jesse's sons would be the next king of Israel. One by one, Samuel saw Jesse's seven oldest sons. But none of them was the one God had chosen.

Samuel asked Jesse, "Do you have any more sons?"

Jesse said, "Yes. David is taking care of the sheep."

Samuel told Jesse to send for him.

David came and stood before Samuel. God told Samuel, "David is the one I have chosen." Samuel poured oil on David's head to show that God wanted him to be the next king of Israel.

Memory Verse
"The Lord is my shepherd, I shall not be in want" (Psalm 23:1).

To Talk About
What did David do for the sheep? What did God choose David to be? God chose you to be his child. How does that make you feel?

Prayer
Thank you, God, for choosing me to be your child. Help me to remember that I am your child and to always do my very best, just as David did. Amen.

David's Sheep

Here are some of David's sheep. But each one has something missing.
Draw the missing part. Then draw some green grass for the sheep to eat.

11.

David and Jonathan

I Samuel 18:1–4; 20

King Saul had a son named Jonathan. Jonathan loved David like a brother. He gave David gifts to show his friendship and loyalty. David loved Jonathan too.

Sometimes King Saul got really angry. Then David played music for him and the king felt better. But Saul was jealous of David. He wanted to kill him.

David asked Jonathan, "Why does the king want to kill me?"

Jonathan did not believe the king wanted to kill David. So David said, "I need you to find out if I am right. I am supposed to eat with the king tomorrow. But I am not going. If the king gets mad, you will know he wants to kill me."

Jonathan said, "Okay. I will meet you in the hills after dinner. I will shoot arrows and send a boy after them. If I tell the boy the arrows are far away, that will mean the king wants to kill you."

When David was not at dinner the next day, King Saul became very angry. He was so angry he threw a spear at Jonathan! Then Jonathan went to the place where David was waiting. Jonathan shot the arrows. He told the boy they were far away.

David came out from his hiding place. Jonathan was very sad. "You must go far away," Jonathan said to David. "But we will always be friends."

Memory Verse
"A friend loves at all times" (Proverbs 17:17).

To Talk About
Why was David afraid? How did Jonathan show that he was David's good friend? How can you be a good friend to someone?

Prayer
Jesus, you are my best friend. I love you. Help me to be a good friend to other people too, just as Jonathan was to David. Amen.

Find the Friends

David and Jonathan were best friends. They loved each other. Can you find the children that are being good friends in these pictures? Color the heart by those children.

12.

Elijah Trusts God

I Kings 17:1–16

King Ahab did not obey God. God told Elijah to take a message to Ahab. Elijah said to Ahab, "You have done many bad things. So God is not going to send any more rain until I say so." King Ahab blamed Elijah because there was no rain. He wanted to hurt Elijah. But Elijah trusted God to help.

God told Elijah to hide by a little stream. Elijah drank water from the stream. And every morning and night, God sent ravens with food for Elijah. God took care of Elijah.

After a while, the stream dried up because there was no rain. Now God told Elijah to go to a faraway town where a woman would help him. Elijah trusted God and did what he said. When Elijah got to the town, he saw the woman. She was picking up sticks. Elijah said, "Please bring me some water and a piece of bread."

The woman was sad. She said, "I don't have any bread. I have just a little flour and some oil. I am gathering sticks to make one last meal for me and my son. When that is gone, we will die."

Elijah said, "Don't be afraid. Go home and do what you said. But first, make me some bread. God will give you flour and oil until it rains again."

The woman did what Elijah said. Elijah, the woman, and her son had food every day. God took care of them.

Memory Verse
"Trust in the LORD" (Psalm 4:5b).

To Talk About
How did God take care of Elijah? What happened to the woman's flour and oil? How does God help you get the food you need?

Prayer
Dear God, thank you giving me food and the other things I need. Help me to trust you, just as Elijah did. Amen.

Growing Things

God provides food for us. One way he does this is by making plants grow. It's fun to see how plants get leaves and roots.

What you need:
sweet potato with buds
glass jar
toothpicks

What you do:
1. Fill a glass jar with water. Stick toothpicks into the bigger end of the sweet potato to keep it from falling into the jar.

2. Put the sweet potato into the jar with the smaller end down. Be sure the bottom of the sweet potato is in the water. Check the water every day so that the bottom of the potato is always wet.

3. Set the sweet potato in a sunny place. Watch the roots grow down and green leaves grow up.

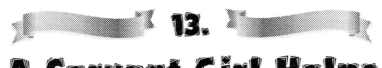

13.

A Servant Girl Helps

2 Kings 5:1-15

Naaman was a leader of a big army in a faraway country. But Naaman got very sick. No one knew how to help him get well.

A servant girl worked in Naaman's house. The girl was kind and wanted to help him. She knew what to do. The girl told Naaman's wife, "Naaman should go and see God's prophet Elisha. God will show Elisha how to help Naaman get well."

Naaman heard what the girl said. So he went to see Elisha. But when Naaman got to Elisha's house, Elisha didn't come out to see him. He sent a message to Naaman. The message said, "Wash in the Jordan River seven times and you will be well."

Naaman was angry. He didn't want to wash in a dirty river. But Naaman's servant said, "Please do what Elisha said."

So Naaman went to the Jordan River. Naaman washed in the river four times. But he didn't get well. Naaman washed in the river three more times. When he came up out of the water the seventh time, Naaman was well.

Naaman thanked God for making him well. He thanked God for the kind servant girl who knew God would help him.

Memory Verse
"Serve one another in love" (Galatians 5:13).

To Talk About
How did the servant girl help Naaman? Who helps you when you need help?

Prayer
Dear God, thank you for taking care of me. Thank you for my parents and others who help me. Help me to be kind and help other people, just as the servant girl helped Naaman.

Being Kind

Who can be kind and help? Draw a line from the helpers to someone or some way they can help.

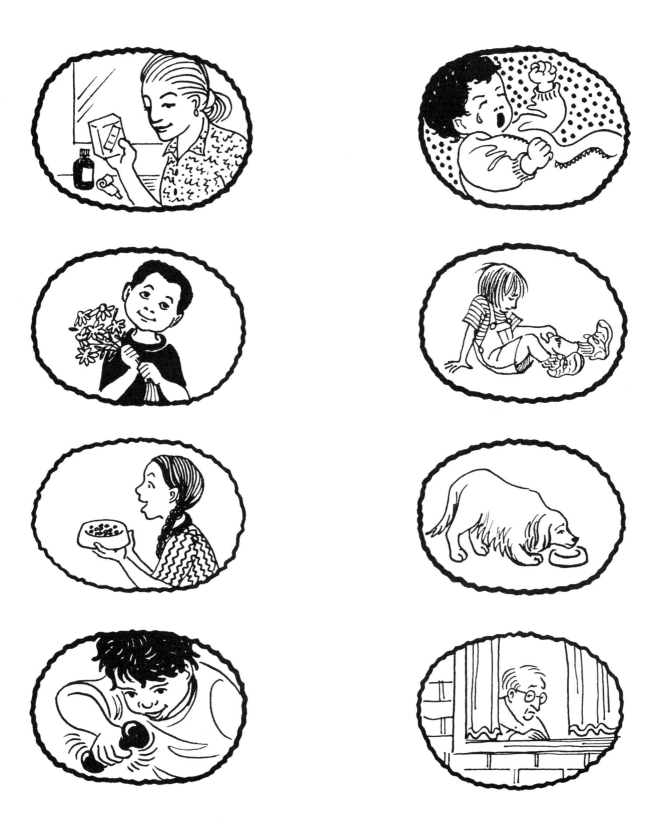

14.

Three Brave Men

Daniel 3

A rich king decided to build a big statue of shiny gold. The king said, "When you hear my special music, all of you must pray to this statue."

All the people came. When they heard the music, they prayed to the statue, except for three men. Shadrach, Meshach, and Abednego loved God. They would pray only to him. The three men stood straight and tall.

This made the king very angry. He called for his soldiers. The king told the soldiers to bring the three men to him. The king said, "I will give you one more chance to bow down to the statue." The men said they loved God and prayed only to him.

The king told the soldiers to make a very hot fire in a big furnace. Then he ordered the soldiers to throw the men into the furnace. The soldiers threw them into the furnace. The king and all the soldiers watched to see what would happen. They couldn't believe what they saw.

Inside the furnace, the three men were walking around. And there was another man with them. He looked like an angel. None of them were burned.

The king walked to the furnace and called, "Your God saved you. Come out." Only three men walked out. They were not burned at all. Their hair and clothes didn't even smell like smoke. God had saved them.

Memory Verse
"You shall have no other gods before me" (Exodus 20:3).

To Talk About
Why didn't the men pray to the statue? How did God help the men? How can you show that you love God?

Prayer
God, I love you. Thank you for all the things you do for me. Amen.

They Loved God

Do the actions in this fingerplay about the three brave men, while an adult or older child reads the words.

A rich king built a big gold statue.	*"Build" from the floor up toward ceiling.*
Everyone was told to pray to the statue.	*Fold hands and bow head.*
The music played.	*Pretend to blow a horn.*
All the people came.	*Walk in place.*
They bowed down in front of the statue.	*Bow down.*
But three men stood up straight and tall.	*Stand as tall as possible.*
They did not pray to the statue.	*Shake head "no."*
The men loved God and prayed to him.	*Point upward and then fold hands.*
The king told the soldiers to make a hot fire.	*"Shovel" coal into furnace.*
They threw the men into the furnace.	*Throw with two hands.*
The king and soldiers looked in the furnace.	*Hand above eyes—looking.*
Were they surprised!	*Look surprised.*
The three men were walking around.	*Walk in place.*
There was another person with them.	*Hold up four fingers.*
He looked like an angel.	*Cross arms over chest.*
The king told the men to come out.	*Jump forward.*
The men didn't even smell like smoke.	*Sniff hands and arms.*
The men loved God and prayed to him.	*Point upward and then fold hands.*
God had saved them.	*Hug yourself.*

15.

The Roaring Lions

Daniel 6

The king chose Daniel to be a ruler over other rulers. The other rulers were jealous of Daniel. They wanted to get Daniel in trouble. But Daniel always did things right.

The rulers knew Daniel prayed to God three times a day. So they made a plan. They said to the king, "Make it a law that everyone may pray only to you for thirty days." The king thought that sounded fine. So the law was made.

Daniel knew about the law. But he kept praying to God each day. He knew that he should pray to God alone.

The rulers saw Daniel praying. Then they ran to tell the king. The king couldn't change the law. So Daniel was thrown into a den of hungry lions for disobeying the law. Daniel wasn't afraid. God gave him courage.

All night the king thought about Daniel trapped in the den with the lions. As soon as it got light, the king ran to the lions' den. The king yelled into the den, "Daniel, did God take care of you?" He was glad when Daniel answered, "I'm fine. God sent an angel. He kept the mouths of the lions shut."

"Bring Daniel out of the lions' den," the king ordered. After that the king told all his people to pray to Daniel's God.

Memory Verse
"Act with courage, and may the LORD be with those who do well" (2 Chronicles 19:11).

To Talk About
What happened when Daniel prayed to God? Who gave courage to Daniel? When does God give you courage?

Prayer
Almighty God, thank you for protecting me. Help me to have courage when I'm scared, just as Daniel did.

Lion Mask

What you need:
white paper plate
yellow paint
paintbrush
orange and brown construction paper
scissors
marker or crayon
glue
yarn
hole punch

What you do:
1. Use the bottom side of the paper plate. Cut out eyeholes. Paint the plate yellow. Let it dry.

2. Cut out three triangles from brown paper. Glue two triangles to the top of the plate for ears. Use the other one for the lion's nose. Draw the lion's mouth with a marker or crayon.

3. Cut out strips of orange paper and glue them around the edge of the plate for the lion's mane.

4. Punch a hole on each side of the mask. Tie a piece of yarn (10–12 inches long) to each hole.

How you can use it:
1. Wear the mask to act out the story of Daniel and the lions.

2. Hang the mask on your wall.

16.
The Big Fish
Jonah 1–3

Jonah was a preacher. His job was to tell people what God said. One day, God told Jonah to go to the big city of Nineveh. God wanted Jonah to tell the people about all the wrong things they were doing.

Jonah did not want to go to Nineveh. He bought a ticket to ride on a ship that was going the other way. Jonah was running away from God.

God made a big storm come on the sea. The sailors were all afraid of the storm. They thought the boat would sink and they would drown. Jonah was sleeping. The captain woke up Jonah. He said, "Pray to your God to save us."

Jonah knew God had sent the storm because he had disobeyed God. Jonah told the sailors, "Throw me in the sea. The storm will stop then."

Kersplash! Jonah was thrown in the water. But God sent a big fish to save Jonah. The fish opened its mouth and swallowed him. Jonah was in the belly of the fish for three days. While he was in the fish, Jonah prayed to God. He was sorry he had disobeyed God.

God heard Jonah's prayer. God made the fish spit Jonah out onto the shore. Jonah obeyed God and went to Nineveh. The people listened to Jonah. They told God they were sorry and God forgave them.

Memory Verse
"I desire to do your will, O my God" (Psalm 40:8a).

To Talk About
How did God save Jonah when he was thrown into the sea? What did Jonah say in his prayer? What should you do when you disobey?

Prayer
Dear God, thank you for forgiving me when I do wrong things. Help me to be sorry when I disobey, just as Jonah was sorry. Amen.

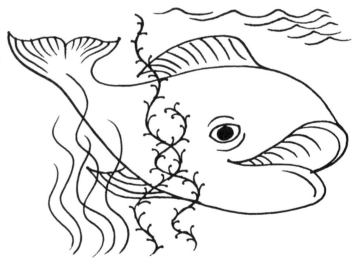

What's Hiding Here?

Color the spaces to see what is hiding.

B = Blue   **Br = Brown**   **Y = Yellow**   **R = Red**

17.

Jesus Is Born

Luke 2:1–20

The king wanted to know how many people lived in the land. Everyone had to go to their hometown to be counted. Mary and Joseph went to the town of Bethlehem. It was a long trip for Mary. She was going to have a baby soon.

Many people had traveled to Bethlehem. All the rooms were full. So Mary and Joseph had to stay in a stable. Mary's baby was born that night. Mary wrapped the baby in strips of cloth. She laid him in a manger. The baby's name was Jesus. Jesus was God's Son.

In the hills near Bethlehem, shepherds were watching their sheep. Suddenly the shepherds saw an angel. They were afraid. The light from the angel was so bright.

The angel said, "Don't be afraid. I have some wonderful news. A Savior has been born in Bethlehem. Go and find him. He's wrapped in strips of cloth and lying in a manger."

Then more and more angels came. They sang praises to God for sending Jesus. Then the angels left. The shepherds hurried to Bethlehem. They found Jesus and were so happy that God had sent his Son. They told everyone they saw that Jesus the Savior had been born.

Memory Verse
"Today . . . a Savior has been born to you" (Luke 2:11).

To Talk About
Where was Jesus born? Who told the shepherds about Jesus? How can you celebrate Jesus' birthday?

Prayer
Loving God, I'm so happy you sent Jesus as my Savior. Help me to praise you and tell others about Jesus, just as the shepherds did. Amen.

The First Christmas

Color this Christmas picture about when baby Jesus was born.

18.

Anna and Simeon

Luke 2:22–40

Mary and Joseph loved baby Jesus. When Jesus was about 40 days old, they made a special trip to the temple in Jerusalem. They wanted to thank God for sending Jesus. They gave a special offering to God.

An old man named Simeon was at the temple. He had been waiting a long time for God to send Jesus. God made a promise to Simeon. God told Simeon that he would not die until he saw Jesus. Simeon saw Mary and Joseph come in. God helped Simeon to know that the baby was Jesus, God's Son. Simeon was excited about seeing the Savior.

Simeon held baby Jesus and praised God. He said, "Lord, you have sent your Son just as you promised. He is the Savior!"

Anna was an old woman who lived at the temple. She loved to worship God. God helped Anna know Jesus was the Savior, too. She thanked God for sending Jesus. She told others that she had seen God's Son.

Mary and Joseph went back to their home. They thought about all that Simeon and Anna had said.

Memory Verse
"I waited patiently for the LORD" (Psalm 40:1a).

To Talk About
Where did Mary and Joseph take Jesus? What did Anna and Simeon do when they saw Jesus? How can you let others know about God's promise to send Jesus?

Prayer
Dear God, thank you for sending your Son as the Savior. Help me to spread the good news about Jesus, just as Anna and Simeon did. Amen.

A Long Wait

Anna and Simeon waited a long, long time for God to send Jesus. They were very patient. Sometimes it's hard to be patient and wait. The things on this page take a long time to happen. Number the pictures in each row. Put 1 by the picture that happened first, 2 by the picture that happened next, and 3 by the picture that happened last.

19.

Special Visitors

Matthew 2:1-12

Some wise men from a faraway country saw a bright star in the sky. "The star will lead us to a new king of God's people," they said. The wise men wanted to worship this new king. They wanted to bring him gifts.

They got on their camels and followed the star across the desert. After a long trip, the wise men came to a big city. They asked, "Where is the new king?" No one knew. The only king the people knew was King Herod.

So the wise men went to see King Herod. He was very angry when he heard about the new king. He wanted to be the only king. Herod asked his helpers to find out where the new king had been born. They told Herod, "God's Word said he was to be born in Bethlehem."

King Herod told the wise men to look for the new king in Bethlehem. Then he lied. He told them to come back after they saw the baby so that he would know where to go to worship him. So the wise men got back on their camels. They followed the star again. It led them to Bethlehem and stopped right over the house where Jesus lived.

The wise men went into the house. They knelt down and worshiped Jesus and gave him their gifts. The gifts showed that they loved Jesus.

In a dream, God told the wise men not to return to King Herod. So the wise men went back home by another road. They were glad they could worship Jesus and give him gifts.

> **Memory Verse**
> "Come, let us bow down in worship" (Psalm 95:6).

To Talk About

How did the wise men find Jesus? How did the wise men show they loved Jesus? How can you show you love Jesus?

Prayer

Jesus, I am so happy you are my Savior. Help me to show my love for you and to worship you, just as the wise men did. Amen.

© In Celebration™   40   IF9560 *Christian Virtues (PreK-K)*

Finding Jesus

Help the wise men find their way to Jesus.

The Boy Jesus

Luke 2:41–52

Mary and Joseph and Jesus lived in Nazareth. That was far from the temple in Jerusalem. So they went there only once a year. When Jesus was 12 years old, he went with Mary and Joseph. They had to walk almost a week. Many other people walked with them.

Jesus went into the temple with his family. They worshiped God. They sang and prayed to God. They gave their offerings to God.

Then Mary and Joseph started back home. They walked all day. That night Mary and Joseph looked around. But they couldn't find Jesus. Mary and Joseph were worried. They went back to Jerusalem to look for Jesus.

Finally, they found Jesus at the temple. He was sitting with the teachers. Jesus was listening to them and asking questions. Mary and Joseph were very surprised. They said, "Jesus, you had us worried."

Jesus said, "Why were you worried? Didn't you know I had to be in my Father's house?" Jesus was talking about God. Jesus knew he was God's Son.

Jesus liked to be in God's house. But he went back to Nazareth with Mary and Joseph. Jesus obeyed Mary and Joseph. God was pleased with Jesus. People were pleased with him too.

Memory Verse
Jesus said, "I had to be in my Father's house" (Luke 2:49).

To Talk About
Why did Jesus like to be in the temple?
Why do you like to go to church?

Prayer
Dear God, I like to go to church and sing and pray. Help me to learn more about you. Amen.

In God's House

Jesus learned about God in the temple. You can learn about God when you go to church. Ask someone to help you sing this song about God's house. Do the actions as you sing.

Sing to the tune of "Mulberry Bush."

I'm so glad to go to church,　　　　　*Walk in place.*
Go to church, go to church.
I'm so glad to go to church
And learn how much God loves me.　　*Hug yourself.*

When I'm in church I sing and pray,　*Hold hands open like a book; hold together to pray.*
Sing and pray, sing and pray.
When I'm in church I sing and pray
And tell God how much I love him.　　*Point upward.*

I am God's very special child,　　　　*Point upward and then to yourself.*
Special child, special child.　　　　　*Point to yourself.*
I am God's very special child　　　　 *Point upward and then to yourself.*
So I will thank and praise him.　　　　*Turn around with both hands in the air.*

© In Celebration™

IF9560 *Christian Virtues (PreK-K)*

21.

Jesus Helps at a Wedding

John 2:1-11

One day Jesus and his disciples went to a wedding. Jesus' mother, Mary, was at the wedding too. The wedding party went on for a long time. Soon the wine was all gone. Mary came to Jesus and said, "They have run out of wine."

Then Mary talked to the servants. She said, "Do whatever Jesus tells you to do."

There were six large stone jars standing by the door. Each of them held lots and lots of water. Jesus told the servants, "Fill these six jars with water." The servants filled them to the top.

Then Jesus said, "Take a cup of water out of one of the jars. Have the man in charge of this wedding feast taste it."

A servant did what Jesus told him to do. As the servant hurried to the man in charge, Jesus changed all the water into wine. When the man in charge tasted the wine, he said to the bridegroom, "Usually people serve the best wine first. But you saved the best until now."

Jesus cared about his friends and their wedding. He wanted to help them and give them what they needed. And he gave them the very best!

Memory Verse
"If one falls down, his friend can help him up" (Ecclesiastes 4:10).

To Talk About
Jesus helped his friends at a wedding by turning water into wine. How can you help someone?

Prayer
Dear Jesus, thank you for being my friend and always helping me. Help me to be kind and helpful, just like you. Amen.

Six Stone Jars

Trace the dotted lines to make the six stone jars. Then color the picture.

22.

One Said Thanks

Luke 17:11-19

Ten men were sitting by a road near a town. They were very sick with leprosy. The doctors could not make them better. The men could not live at home with their families. They had to live by themselves so other people would not get sick. The ten men felt very lonely and sad.

One day the men saw Jesus coming down the road. They called to him, "Jesus, please help us!" Jesus heard the men and stopped to talk with them. The sick men trusted Jesus. They believed he could make them well.

Jesus told the men, "Go to the priests. They will see if you are healed."

On the way to see the priests, the ten men were made well. They were so happy! Now they could live at home again. Nine of the men ran home. They did not stop to thank Jesus for making them well.

But one man stopped and came back. "Thank you, Jesus, for making me well," he said.

Jesus asked the man, "Where are the other nine men? Are you the only one to return and praise God?"

Jesus paused. "Go home now. You were made well because you believed in me."

The man was glad he said thank you to Jesus.

Memory Verse
"Give thanks to the LORD, for he is good" (Psalm 136:1).

To Talk About
Why didn't all the sick men thank Jesus? What are some things for which you can thank Jesus?

Prayer
Dear Jesus, you give me many things. Help me to remember to say "Thank you" just as the sick man did. Amen.

Thank-You Place Mat

What you need:
large piece of bright-colored poster board
old magazines
scissors
glue
crayons
clear adhesive paper

What you do:
1. Print "Thank you, God" with big letters in the center of the poster board.

2. Cut pictures out of magazines of the things God gives you. You can cut out such things as food, clothes, people, pets, and houses.

3. Glue the pictures around the words.

4. Cover the board with clear adhesive paper, such as Con-Tact.

How you can use it:
1. Use it as a place mat to help you remember to thank God for everything.

2. Use it as a poster to hang on your wall.

23.

God Cares for Us

Matthew 6:25–34

Jesus went to a mountain to talk to his disciples. Many other people came to see Jesus. Jesus sat down and the people sat around him. They wanted to hear all that he had to say.

Jesus told the people to look up in the sky. They could see birds flying around and singing happily. Jesus said, "See those birds. They are happy and safe. God feeds the birds and gives them what they need. You don't need to worry about what you will eat and drink either. You are more important to God than the birds. He will take care of you."

Then Jesus asked the people to look all around. They could see beautiful purple, pink, and yellow flowers blooming on the mountain. Jesus said, "God gave the flowers their beautiful colors. He has given them what they need. You don't need to worry about clothes. You are more important to God than flowers. He will take care of you. God will give you everything that you need."

Through Jesus' teachings, we learn that God loves us very much. He loves us more than the birds and the flowers. We are very important to God. He takes good care of us.

Memory Verse
"[God] cares for you" (1 Peter 5:7).

To Talk About
How does God take care of the birds and flowers? How does God care for you?

Prayer
Dear God, there are many beautiful birds and flowers in the world. Thank you for taking care of them. Thank you for taking care of me too. Help me to tell others about your love, just as Jesus did.

Bird Feeders

What you need:
½ gallon milk carton
string
tempera paints
paintbrush
scissors
birdseed

What you do:
1. Cut out large windows on all sides of the milk carton. Leave two inches, top and bottom.

2. Paint the milk carton.

3. Poke two holes through the top of the carton. Tie the string through each hole.

4. Fill the bottom of the carton with birdseed.

How you can use it:
Hang the feeder by the strings from a tree limb. Place it where you can watch the birds eat. Remember to add birdseed every few days.

24.
The Good Samaritan
Luke 10:25-37

Jesus wanted to teach the people to be kind and to help others. So he told this story. A Jewish man was going to the city of Jericho. He had to travel along a lonely road. All of a sudden, some robbers jumped out from behind the rocks. The robbers beat the man until he was almost dead. Then they took his money and everything else he had. They left the man lying along the side of the road.

Soon a priest from the temple came walking down the road. He walked right by the hurt man. But the priest did not stop to help. Next a Levite walked down the road. The Levite saw the hurt man, but he too passed by without stopping.

Then a Samaritan man came by. Jews and Samaritans did not like each other. But the Samaritan felt sorry for the hurt man, so he stopped to help. He washed the blood and dirt from the man. The Samaritan let the hurt man ride his donkey. He took the man to an inn and cared for him.

In the morning, the Samaritan gave some money to the man who owned the inn. "Take care of him until I come back," the Samaritan said to the innkeeper.

Memory Verse
"Love your neighbor as yourself"
(Luke 10:27).

To Talk About
What happened to the man? How did the Samaritan help? How can you be kind and helpful to someone?

Prayer
Dear Jesus, I like to hear the stories you told to teach us important lessons. Help me to be like the Samaritan by being kind and helping others. Amen.

The One Who Helped

Draw a line down the road the Samaritan needs to follow to get the hurt man to the inn.

25.

Stopping a Storm

Mark 4:35–41

Jesus was very tired. All day long he had talked about God and helped many people. He had made sick people well. Now it was almost nighttime. Jesus said to his disciples, "Let's go across the lake."

So Jesus and his disciples got into a boat and started across the lake. Jesus lay down in the back of the boat. Soon he was sound asleep.

When the boat was almost in the middle of the lake, the wind began to blow. It blew harder and harder. The waves got bigger and bigger. Water began to splash into the boat. But Jesus kept right on sleeping.

Jesus' disciples were very afraid. The men thought the boat would sink and they would all drown. The disciples called out, "Wake up, Jesus! Don't you care if we drown?"

Jesus woke up. Then he spoke to the wind and the waves. Jesus said, "Quiet! Be still!"

Right away, the storm was over. The wind stopped and the waves went down. Everything was quiet and peaceful. Jesus looked at his disciples. He asked them, "Why were you afraid? Don't you have faith in me?"

The disciples were surprised by what happened. They said, "Even the wind and waves obey Jesus."

Memory Verse
"Peace I leave with you; my peace I give you" (John 14:27).

To Talk About
Why were Jesus' disciples afraid? What are some things that make you afraid? Jesus can help you when you are afraid.

Prayer
Dear Jesus, thank you for knowing when I am afraid. Help me to feel peaceful and safe, just as your disciples felt after the storm. Amen.

Wave Bottle

What you need:
1 plastic 2-liter soda bottle
water
cooking oil
blue food coloring
tiny plastic boat (optional)

What you do:
1. Fill the bottle 3/4 full of water.

2. Add several drops of blue food coloring to the water.

3. Fill the rest of the bottle with oil. Pour the oil into the water very slowly. Close very tightly.

4. Hold the bottle horizontally and tip the bottle from side to side.

How you can use it:
1. Tell the story of Jesus and the storm. Shake the bottle to make the waves. Stop shaking the bottle to show peaceful waters.

2. Put a tiny plastic boat in the bottle. Watch it bounce around on the waves when you shake the bottle.

26.

I Can See!

Mark 10:46–52

Bartimaeus was a blind man. Every day he sat beside the road just outside the town of Jericho. He couldn't see anything, but he could hear people walking by. Bartimaeus begged for money from all the people who passed.

One day Bartimaeus heard a big crowd walking along the road. He asked the people, "What's happening?"

"Jesus is coming," they answered.

Bartimaeus called out to Jesus. Bartimaeus believed Jesus could help him. He began to shout, "Jesus, please help me!"

Many people told Bartimaeus to be quiet. But Bartimaeus would not be quiet. He shouted even louder, "Jesus! Please have mercy on me!"

Jesus stopped when he heard Bartimaeus. "Bring him to me," Jesus said.

So the people called to the blind man, "Cheer up! On your feet! Jesus is calling you." Bartimaeus jumped to his feet and came to Jesus.

"What do you want me to do for you?" Jesus asked him.

Bartimaeus said, "Jesus, I want to see."

"Go," said Jesus, "You believe in me, so now you can see." Right away, Bartimaeus could see. He was not blind anymore.

Bartimaeus thanked God and followed Jesus along the road.

Memory Verse
"Be strong in the Lord and in his mighty power" (Ephesians 6:10).

To Talk About
Bartimaeus did not give up. He kept calling to Jesus. What did Jesus do for Bartimaeus? How can you call to Jesus for help?

Prayer
Dear God, thank you for hearing my prayers. Help me to not give up and to keep on praying to you, just as Bartimaeus did. Amen.

"Feely" Bag

Bartimaeus was blind. He could not see anything. But he could hear. He listened carefully to know what was happening. Blind people also use their hands to feel things in order to tell what they are. Play this game to guess what things are without seeing them.

What you need:
a grocery bag or other bag you can't see through
small items—piece of fruit, toy, rock, sock, comb, ball, spoon
scarf or towel to use as a blindfold

What you do:
1. Have someone choose the items and put them in the bag.
2. Put on the blindfold or close your eyes tight.
3. Reach in the bag and feel an item. Tell what you think it is.
4. Pull it out to see if you were right.

What do you like to see? Draw a picture of it in this box.

27.

Up in a Tree

Luke 19:1–10

Zacchaeus was a tax collector, but he didn't always treat people fairly. He made people pay more tax money than they owed. Then Zacchaeus kept some of the money for himself. He had a lot of money, but he didn't have many friends.

One day, Zacchaeus heard Jesus was coming to his town. He had heard all about Jesus and really wanted to see him. But there were lots of people who came to see Jesus. Zacchaeus was very short. He could not see over all the people. No one would let him stand in the front.

Then Zacchaeus had an idea. He climbed up into a big tree that leaned out over the road. Now he could see.

Just then, Jesus was walking under the tree. He stopped and looked right up at Zacchaeus! Jesus said to him, "Zacchaeus, come down from that tree! I must stay at your house today." Zacchaeus came down at once. He was so happy that Jesus was coming to his house.

All the people saw this and began to say, "Jesus is with a bad man."

But Zacchaeus was sorry for what he had done. He said to Jesus, "I will give half of everything I have to poor people. And if I have taken too much tax money from some people, I will pay back four times as much."

Jesus said to him, "I came to help people like you change."

Memory Verse
"He wanted to see . . . Jesus" (Luke 19:3).

To Talk About
What did Zacchaeus do to see Jesus? How did Zacchaeus feel when Jesus said he was going to his house? How did Zacchaeus change?

Prayer
Thank you, Jesus, for being my friend. When I have problems, help me to figure out what to do, just as Zacchaeus did. Amen.

Where's Zacchaeus?

Zacchaeus wanted to see Jesus so much that he climbed up in a tree. Which path will take Jesus to the tree where Zacchaeus is sitting? Use a crayon to go over the right path.

28.

Hosanna to Jesus!

Luke 19:28-38; John 12:13

Jesus and his disciples were going to Jerusalem. When they came to the Mount of Olives, Jesus called two of his disciples to him. He said, "Go to the village ahead of you. You will find a young donkey tied up there. Untie it and bring it to me. Someone will ask you why you are taking the donkey. Tell him the Lord needs it."

The two men went and found the donkey, just as Jesus said. As they were untying the donkey, the owners asked, "Why are you untying the donkey?" The disciples said, "The Lord needs it." The owners did not stop them.

The disciples brought the donkey to Jesus. They threw their coats on the donkey's back. Jesus got on the donkey and rode toward Jerusalem. As he went along, people spread their coats on the road.

As they traveled down the road, a big crowd began to joyfully praise Jesus in loud voices. They took palm branches and went out to meet him, shouting "Hosanna! Blessed is he who comes in the name of the Lord! Blessed is the King of Israel!"

The people were happy to see Jesus. They treated him like a king.

Memory Verse
"Hosanna! . . . Blessed is the King of Israel!" (John 12:13).

To Talk About
How did the people praise Jesus? What are some ways you can praise Jesus?

Prayer
Dear Jesus, you really are the king of the whole world. Help me to always praise you, just as the people along the road to Jerusalem did. Amen.

Praise Parade

The people praised Jesus when he came riding into Jerusalem. You can make some things to praise Jesus and have your own parade.

What you need:
2 white paper plates
dried beans, small stones, or unpopped corn
crayons or markers
stapler
scissors
green construction paper
green plastic tape, cut into small pieces

What you do:
1. Print "Hosanna" on the back side of both plates. Decorate the plates with crayons or markers.

2. Put some beans, stones, or corn on the undecorated side of one plate.

3. Place the other plate on top and staple them together around the edges. Make sure the staples are close enough together so that the beans (or other items) do not fall out.

4. Cut a leaf shape from the green paper.

5. Stick pieces of green tape on the leaf to look like veins.

How you can use it:
Have a praise parade with your family and friends. Shake the paper plate tambourines, wave the palms, and shout "Hosanna!"

29.

Washing Feet

John 13:1-17

Jesus knew that soon he would have to die on the cross. So he wanted to show his special love to his disciples. Jesus decided to wash their feet. This was a dirty job, and usually a servant did it.

While the evening meal was being served, Jesus got up from the table. He took off his outer clothes and wrapped a towel around his waist. After that, he poured water into a big bowl and began to wash his disciples' feet. He dried them with the towel that was wrapped around him. The disciples did not know what to say. Peter did not like Jesus washing his feet. He said, "No, Jesus, I don't want you to wash my feet. Let me wash yours."

Jesus answered, "Now you do not know why I am doing this. But later you will understand. Unless I wash you, you have no part with me."

"Then, Jesus," Peter said, "not just my feet but my hands and my head too!" Peter did not understand, so Jesus explained it to him. "You have had a bath, so only your feet are dirty. The rest of you is clean."

When Jesus had finished washing their feet, he put on his clothes and returned to the table. Jesus explained, "Now that I have washed your feet, you should also wash one another's feet. You should do as I have done for you." Jesus wanted them to serve one another.

Memory Verse
"Serve one another in love" (Galatians 5:13).

To Talk About
Why did Jesus wash his disciples' feet? Jesus wanted his disciples to serve each other. How can you serve others?

Prayer
Jesus, thank you for loving me. Help me to love others and serve them, just as you served your disciples. Amen.

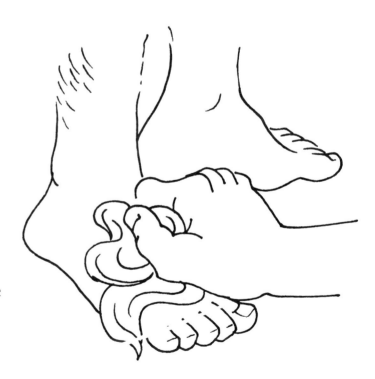

Serving Others

Jesus wanted to show his disciples how much he loved them. So he served them by washing their feet. Some of the things from the story are hidden in the border around this picture. Find: a big bowl, some water, a towel, three feet, and Jesus' coat. Circle the things and then color the picture.

© In Celebration™ IF9560 *Christian Virtues (PreK-K)*

30.

Happy Day!

Luke 24:1-10

Jesus had died on a cross. His body had been placed in a tomb. A big rock had been rolled in front of the opening. Some of the women watched as Jesus was buried. They wanted to come back later.

Very early Sunday morning, just as the sun was coming up, the women went to the tomb. They carried sweet-smelling ointments and spices to put on Jesus' body. They wondered how they would roll away the big stone.

But when the women got there, the stone had been rolled away. They went into the tomb, but the body of Jesus was not there. What had happened to his body?

Suddenly two angels stood beside them. The angels' clothes gleamed like lightning. The women were so scared, they bowed down with their faces on the ground.

The angels said to them, "Why are you looking for Jesus among the dead? He is not here; he has risen! Jesus told you that he would be crucified and on the third day be raised again." Then they remembered what Jesus said.

The women were so happy! They ran to tell all of Jesus' disciples what had happened. "Jesus has risen! He is alive!" they said.

Memory Verse
"He is not here; he has risen!"
(Luke 24:6).

To Talk About

What did the angels say to the women?
How did the women show they were happy?
How can you show you are happy?

Prayer

Risen Jesus, I am so happy you rose from the dead. Help me to tell others the joyful news, just as the women did. Amen.

joyfulness

Wonderful News!

The women were very happy when they heard the wonderful news that Jesus was alive. Add happy smiles to the faces of the women. You can also draw some flowers, the sun, and the big stone that was rolled away. When you are finished drawing, color the picture.

Notes